Life with God

Encouraging and inspiring new believers to

do life with God

The new believer's devotional that encourages and

inspires a changed life.

Shakira L. Thomas

Life with God

Copyright ©2018 Shakira L. Thomas

All scripture quotations in this publication are from the Good News Translation in Today's English Version, Second Edition Copyright ©1992 by American Bible Society. Used by Permission.

ISBN-13: 978-1-79216-991-5

Dedication

This book is dedicated to God, my Father, my everything. I am nothing without you Lord and everything I should be with you. I am living my best life because of you. Growing, maturing and becoming the woman, you destined me to be. Thank you, Father, I love you and this is for your honor and glory.

Contents

Introduction

I remember the season in my life, when I came to the realization that I need Jesus. I had reached a critical point in my life and needed a reset. I was exhausted mentally, physically, emotionally, and spiritually. The thought of seeking guidance from my support system or pursue my own agenda no longer made any sense to me. I needed more than a hearty talk, a vacation to unwind or pursue my own wisdom. I needed someone bigger than me, my family and friends. Then just like that, it hit me like a ton of bricks, it is God who I need. The One who made me. I needed my Papa, my Father, my Creator. The One who knows me more than I know myself, loves me unconditionally and wants to help me. The One who knows the combinations to open me and fix me. The only One who has the blueprint on me, and who could restore, realign me, and set me right. No one can do that only Jesus.

I remember being very emotional yet ready to unload my burdens to Jesus. Captivated by who He is to me and how he can restore me. Then I felt the Lord impressed on me to just let it all out to Him. I did that for days, just crying and emptying out my heart to Him. Then a hunger and thirst for His word (the bible) erupt in the womb of my soul – and I surrendered. Daily I sat before Jesus feet, read the Bible, fasted and surrendered my carnal ways in exchange for his righteousness. My life changed instantly, now God is at work in me. No more doing things my way, depending on my feelings and wisdom. Then I noticed the more I surrender to Him, obey His instructions, humble myself the more fulfilling and fruitful my life is becoming. It was then I find peace and closure to my life struggles and resolution to the constant conflicts with people. It was then that I started loving myself, seeing my beauty and accepting who I am. It was then that I understood how I got here, realized my purpose in life and experience the happiness and contentment for which we are all searching. Before Christ I used to do things based on how I feel and my mere wisdom which have often detour me from God's will for me. Now that I trust the leading of the Holy Spirit, my life is now in line with God's will and His blessings and favors is upon me. I don't worry when problems come, I simply trust and obey God's instructions on defeating the issue. I am his child and He is my Father and He loves me with an everlasting love.

In this book, I share my journey as a new believer to a now mature Christian who continues to do life with God. My purpose for telling my story is to demonstrate the hand of God in my life and to give you hope of what he can do in yours if you allow Him. At the same time, I would like to inspire unbelievers to give Jesus a chance.

Who am I? I am a child of God. I believe in Jesus Christ, the Savior of this world, and the Holy Spirit of God who lives in me and leads me. My purpose in the Kingdom of God is to teach about salvation in Christ, as well as encourage and inspire my fellow believers to continue to do life with God.

Lord, thank You for loving me unconditionally; thank

You for bringing me back to You, for making me all Yours.

Thank You for the opportunity to share with others Your gift

of salvation. I thank You, God, for all those who read this book

who will never be the same. For those who are not yet

believers, as they read this book, stir the beginnings of the

conversion process in each heart. For believers who are facing

challenges, I pray my story will encourage, inspire and

catapult their faith to the next level. I pray that as believers

we will always be patient with ourselves and remember that

we are all going through the sanctification process. LORD, I

give You all the glory and the praise. I lift up Your name high.

I praise You. You are King of kings and Lord of all lords; You

are supreme. There is and never will be anyone like You. I

love You, Daddy, and this book is for

You! Amen.

Preface

Sometime, during my conversion season, God impressed upon me that one day I will share my story, to encourage other believers, who are going through what I overcame. He inspired on my spirit, *'you will share your story of how I am with you and how I transformed you, encourage them and let them know that I will do the same if they trust me'*. God speaks to me on a number of occasions about things of my life, through visions or impressing my spirit and the Lord words always come to pass.

At the time when God shared this piece of information with me, I remember just saying *'Oh'* with a little fear in my heart but then He assured me that I will be ready when the time comes. Six years later, and He has fully prepared me for such a time as this and there is no shadow of fear in me anymore. You see, during those years God has been transforming me, teaching, working out things in me to get me to this point where I am bold, confident and can discern his instructions. You will see this very process throughout my story, every experience in this book has the hand of God all over it. I pray you will be blessed by it.

In Christ

"I am the way, the truth and the life; no one goes to

the Father except by me."

(John 14:6)

"If you're not living for God, you're living for Satan." This statement changed my life some years ago! I remember my response: "Oh, no! I am not living for Satan. Are you crazy?!" Hearing this forced me to really take inventory of my life and relationship with God. I thought, *but how can that be? That's just not truth! I may not be going to church every week or be the most righteous and holy person, but I'm not serving the devil!* Your response would probably be along that same line. "I'm a good, kind and helpful person; I donate clothing to the Salvation Army and give away food to the homeless. My family can always count on me because I'm a caring and compassionate person, so how can I be doing all that good and be living for Satan?" Friends, while all of that is good, if you have not accepted Jesus Christ as your personal Savior and been baptized in the Holy Spirit, you fall under the family of Satan.

Two families exist in this world—Adam's family and Christ's family. Who is Adam? He is the head of the human race, the first human being God created; and we are his descendants. When God created Adam, you and I were also created; we were in Adam—all the billions of us who have ever lived, including Eve. When God made Eve, He never returned to the dust to do so; instead, He went into Adam's side and took out his rib to make Eve (Genesis 2:21). So when God was talking to Adam in the garden, He was really talking to all of mankind who would follow Adam; and in Genesis 3:16, when God told Eve childbearing would be difficult for her, He was talking to all women—and that is the reality still today. Every mother can attest to the pains of childbirth. Mankind is all the same, very much like Adam. Adam disobeyed God, and you and I also disobey God. We share Adam's character and issues. We knew God, but disobedience made us spiritually dead and disconnected us from Him; and now we are all under the judgment of God.

God is our Creator and Maker (Genesis 1:1). God made us in His image (Genesis 1:26) and created us to take charge and dominate earth with Him. That, my friend, is the key purpose of human beings—to "do" life with God. Anything outside of that purpose is confusion, brokenness and evil, much like we are seeing in the world today. God is righteous and perfect; He is the definition of love, and He is truth and light (1 John 1:5). So, when Adam and Eve, who were like God (full of righteousness), allowed the prince of darkness (Satan) to cause them to disobey (Genesis 3:5), they immediately lost their connection to God and became carnal. God is righteous and holy and can occupy only where there is righteousness. Adam and Eve could no longer hear from God or be led by Him, because they became carnal—rebellious, jealous, prideful, selfish, evil, self-righteous, self-independent (Colossians 2:13)—and Satan became their ruler. Satan is the leader of the people who disobey God. The history of mankind is the story of Adam's family, a family into which we were all born. If you still have doubts about the judgment we receive after disconnection from God, read the story of Cain and Abel, the first set of descendants of Adam and Eve (Genesis 4:1-12). Cain killed his brother Abel because of greed and jealousy. How different is our world today from that first murder? Not much different, right? We still see the same evil. When we disobeyed God, we became spiritually dead and carnal and the prince of darkness, Satan, became our leader and led us astray, far from God.

But God loves us so much that He was never going to leave us in the sinful, lost, blind, condemned state we inherited; in fact, God (who is all knowing) knew that we were going to destroy the perfect life we had with Him. So, from eternity past, He made plans for us to come back to Him. God is a good

4

Father! God sent His only Son, Jesus (John 3:16), to come to earth in human form to pay for our disobedience and bring us back into a relation with God (John 3:17). Before Christ, mankind hardly had a relationship with God because of carnality; Satan was leading them astray, only a few men and women desired to know God—men like Abraham, Moses, Esther and David. They wanted to do life with God.

In the Old Testament, God used a substitution system to cover sin. Our ancestors had to shed the blood of innocent animals to cover their sins and make them able to go before the Lord. It was a cleansing ritual that acted as purification. Since God is righteous with no darkness in Him, we also have to be cleansed in order to approach God. God did away with this system of animal sacrifices when He sent Jesus, His son, who knew no sin yet became sin so that we might be made righteous (1 Corinthians 5:21). "Why blood?" you might ask. The Bible says the wages of sin is death (Romans 6:23)—spiritual death; physical death would eventually follow. This penalty of sin would cause a life to be taken, hence the killing of animals to atone for sin. Sin always required a sacrifice. Jesus is our final and ultimate sacrifice. He paid for our sins through the remission of blood in return for a new spirit, His spirit, that brings us back into connection with God.

The result of what Jesus Christ did for us is more powerful than the sin of Adam according to Romans 5:17, which says, *"But how much greater is the result of what was done by the one man, Jesus Christ! All who receive God's abundant grace and are freely put right with him will rule in life through Christ."* The Bible refers to Jesus as the second Adam (1 Corinthians 15:47). Jesus fixed the mess that Adam brought on us. Do you believe this? I hope you do, because even the demons that plague your life believe (James 2:19). Through Jesus, Satan and all his demons have lost control over your life; they no longer have the power to hold you in disobedience and out of God's beautiful will. If you believe that God pardoned you and gave you this gift of salvation in Jesus, then you must be baptized in the Holy Spirit

6

and become part of the family of Christ. When you repent of your sins and trust in the substitutionary death of Christ on your behalf, then you become "born again." You become a new person in Christ and a new heir of God (John 3-3:6). The split second you believe this, the Holy Spirit then baptizes you and places you in the body of Christ. Through His death He purged, cancelled and paid for your sins. We are forgiven and redeemed, which makes us guiltless, righteous and blameless before God. We have inherited the spiritual blessing of sonship, which includes the gift of eternal life. This is the only way to be reconnected to God—then and only then will we become part of the family of Christ.

Are you struggling with guilt and shame? Are there things that took place in your life for which you just can't forgive yourself or from which you can't move on? Every so often, it comes back to your mind and puts you in a discouraging, dark space. You have issues that are holding you in bondage even right now, and you don't know how to cope. Voices in your head are telling you that you don't have what it takes to do something and because of that you are at the same level, making no progress. Or maybe you are going through a tough time in life when you can hardly make ends meet and your family is dysfunctional. Perhaps you are turning to the entertainment of the world like sex, partying, drinking or the spell of social media to distract you from the issues. You know you don't want to go down that path, but you also don't even know where to start to get out of that lifestyle.

Have you not heard the good news? Why are you staying in that dark, sorrowful state of mind? Have you not heard that Christ can free you from all of that mess? Jesus is the answer to your brokenness, emptiness and loneliness. He can give you a new start. You don't have to go through life alone and figure out everything by yourself. The Holy Spirit wants to help you; He wants to show you what mere eyes cannot see and bless you. He desires to pour out His favor in every area of your life, open doors that have been closed, and set you free from family curses, strongholds and bondages. All it takes is repenting to Jesus and believing that He died and paid for your sins to make you a new person in Him. How simple and beautiful is that?

You may have done some things in your life that you feel are so bad that your life is over and done. Oh, no! Don't believe those lies from Satan. Come to Jesus and receive *forgiveness* instead. When you become a follower of Christ, all sins are forgiven, no matter how big, small, medium or large they are — you are forgiven. Whether you committed the sin last night or a decade ago, you are forgiven. Our heavenly Daddy made it clear in Colossians 1:14 when He said, *"For who the son has set free is free indeed."* No sin is so big that God cannot forgive. It doesn't matter what the sin is; God will forgive you. All you need to do is confess, repent and ask for forgiveness and receive the forgiveness. So many of us find it so hard to believe that we are forgiven and receive forgiveness. Instead, we hold on to the sin and try to logically accept it, creating excuses and reasons;

but doing that is like harboring garbage. Eventually you will start to smell like the garbage, which only makes the problem worse. Let go of your sin and receive God's forgiveness. You can be free! When you say yes to Jesus, you are instantly *reunited to God*. Before Christ, we were out of God and in the world with Satan and his demons doing all manner of things; but Christ paid for our punishment and became the bridge to reconnect us to God. Once you accept Him, you are His child. You can call him *Father, Papa, Daddy* because you have spiritually reunited with Him.

Many unbelievers mistakenly believe that God is everyone's Heavenly Father, but that isn't true. John 6:42, 47 makes that clear: *"Jesus said to them, 'If God really were your Father, you would love me, because I came from God and now I am here. I did not come on my own authority, but he sent me...He who comes from God listens to God's words. You, however, are not from God and that is why you will not listen."*

This means if you do not believe in Jesus Christ, you cannot call God your Father because you do not do as He says.

Believers have *eternal life* in Christ and eternal life with God. 1 John 5:12 says, *"The testimony is this: God has given us eternal life and this life has its source in his son."* When judgment day comes after we leave this world, only those who believe in Jesus and live life with God will have eternal life. I personally believe that *you have not properly planned for the future until you include life after death.* As children in Christ, we have eternal life with God in heaven—that's definitely something to look forward to. *We are free* from the law of sin and death according to Romans 8:2, which says, *"For the law of the spirit, which brings us life in union with Christ Jesus, has set me free from the law of sin and death."* As part of Adam's family, mankind is under the judgment of law, sin and death; we are living in sin, and we will die in sin. But when we are in Christ, we know God and the Holy Spirit guides us—and when we do leave this earth, we and all others who are in Christ will spend eternity in Heaven.

When you become a follower of Christ, *you are justified*. Jesus took upon himself your punishment of death for sin by dying on the cross, which paid God's judgment for your sin. In other words, your debts were all cleared up. You are free from guilt and the penalty of sin. No more must you live your life ashamed over something you did years ago; your debt has been reconciled. Walk boldly in Christ because Jesus has justified you! (See 1 Corinthians 5:21.)

In Christ *you are sanctified*, made holy, set apart for God's use, separate from sin. I don't know about you, but it is my desire to be a whole, complete woman in Christ. Through Christ, my weaknesses can no longer control me; I will have complete control over my body through the Spirit, resist negative thoughts and live a righteous life. That is what you receive when you believe in Christ; you are sanctified and made holy every day.

The moment you become a believer, you *receive the seal* with God's stamp of ownership on you through the Holy Spirit according to Ephesians 1:13, which says, *"And you also became God's people when you heard the true message, the Good News that brought you salvation. You believe in Christ and God put his stamp of ownership on you by giving you the Holy Spirit he had promised."* The Holy Spirit is the Spirit of God. You need the Holy Spirit to guide you through life, break bondages, show you how to walk into your destiny and sanctify you, making you look more like Jesus.

You are complete with Jesus. (See Colossians 2:9-10.) We have everything we need; we are not lacking anything. In Christ, we become one with Him. How beautiful is it that Jesus has complete authority on earth and in heaven, and since all power is in Christ, that means it's in me as well. (See Ephesians 3:20.) Being in Christ, we become the *saints* God made us to be in the first place, righteous and holy through Christ Jesus.

We need God in order to truly live a bountiful life as individuals and as a people. How can we live without God, our Maker? It's not feasible! If you are honest, you'll admit that even though you have all the things you desire in this world, you still feel an emptiness inside when you don't have God as your foundation. Money, spouse, children, career and friends can't seem to fill the emptiness inside. Can I tell you they never ever will because they were never created to complete us; things and people are only blessings.

Everything God created has to stay connected to where He put it in order to live—fish must stay in the water and trees must be in the ground. Land animals won't survive living in water or in the air; they weren't created to live like that, and if they try to live someplace other than where God intended, they will die. It's the same for mankind; we were created to do life with God. Anything outside of that is darkness, brokenness and confusion—which is easy to see in both individuals and the world as a whole. We must be connected to God to survive.

God loves us, and even when we were not thinking about Him, He was thinking about us. God knew we were going to disobey Him. He can see the ending to this fall because He is

God. It was never God's plan to leave us in the darkness for Satan to destroy us. He sent Jesus to save us and bring us back to Him, our Source, because we are a disaster without Him, doing all sorts of evil. Jesus Christ is the way to get back to God.

For Your Quiet Time

Read chapters 1 through 6 in Genesis.

1. Based on your understanding about the two different families in the world, which family are you under? Adam or Christ? Explain why you think you belong to a particular family.

_____

_____

_____

_____

_____

_____

2. As a believer, it is important that you understand the basics of the faith, both for yourself and so that you can share that faith with others. In your own words, explain the story of Adam's disobedience and Christ saving us. (This will help to ensure you understand

what you believe and give you confidence for sharing.)

_____

_____

_____

_____

_____

_____

3. List the nine believers' positions that the Bible says you
receive when you accept Jesus and become a new person in Christ (Hint: You are forgiven! You are justified!
Etc.)

_____

_____

_____

_____

_____

_____

Power Over Spiritual Attacks

"Listen! I have given you authority so that you can walk

on snakes and scorpions and overcome all the

power of the Enemy, and nothing will hurt you."

(Luke 10:19)

We all struggle in this area, whether you understand or believe it or not. I first encountered spiritual attacks in my teen years. I had just become a Christian and had no knowledge of such a thing at the time. I just thought I was an unlucky person who didn't have what it took to be liked. During my adolescence and early adulthood, I struggled. In high school, I was hated by my peers, supposedly for being "too proper and quiet." I know now that it was more than that; it was a spiritual fight. I could hardly wait to finish high school and become an adult; I thought it was a high school thing. I believed that, once I became an adult and was around mature people like myself, things would be better. Little did I know it was even worse in the real world. The encounters were so strange that I operated in an almost constant daze because of the things that would happen to me. I couldn't understand how I could be experiencing such pain when other people seemed to have it so easy. I remember just despising myself. I thought something was wrong with me and that everybody else was lucky because they didn't face the problems I was facing every single day. I did pray to God about it at the time, and, although it didn't change during that time, I had peace that I should not give up. Still, my thoughts and feelings about myself were sour.

Are you experiencing constant challenges in your life that don't seem to be improving? Perhaps you have not been able to keep a job for some strange reason. Every time you get a job, something always seems to go wrong. Perhaps you've struggled with relationships—maybe even to the point that a marriage has ended. You're concerned because you want to be married and have a family, but you don't know what else to do to make your relationships work. Does it seem that everything you touch falls apart—whether it's going back to school, starting a business, maintaining a relationship—problems just keep happening, one obstacle after another. You feel that something is working against you to prevent you from moving forward. Have you struggled for years with self-loathing? Perhaps you don't understand yourself completely, and the little you do understand, you hate. At the end of the day you feel drained, you feel like you've failed, and you feel like giving up.

In cases like this, many turn to drugs or alcohol to take away the pain, or they get involved with people and activities that are not good for them. And doing so pulls them even further away from the One they really need, and the only One who can help—God, our Father.

Christians also experience obstacles resulting from spiritual attacks. Thankfully, we have the Holy Spirit to help us through. These attacks come from the devil to discourage believers from trusting and believing God, to shatter our faith and derail us from receiving God's blessings. They can have a lasting, even permanent and detrimental effect on us. Spiritual attacks can be in the form of sickness, finances, family problems, marital problems, mental health, gender confusion, an identity crisis — and the list could go on and on. In other words, anything that is pulling us away from pursuing and believing God is a spiritual attack. Satan's ultimate goal is for us to turn our back on our faith and think the worst about ourselves; he wants to isolate us and finish us off. He wants us to have nothing to do with God.

Through the Holy Spirit, Christians can have power over any spiritual attack. One instant transition that took place when we gave our lives to Jesus was the adjustment of our triune nature. We are no longer led by our human nature; instead we are led by our spirit, which is influenced by the Holy Spirit of God. The Holy Spirit lives in us and shares the thoughts and will of God to help us understand God. It is the Holy Spirit that gives us power and authority over things of this earth, including bondages that have been challenging us for years. If you have problems you have been trying to resolve for years, the Holy Spirit will give you the answer. He is your problem solver.

As a new believer in Christ, you may be wondering why you still have problems. Or perhaps you're in the conversion season, but the enemy is trying to get you distracted by throwing disappointments, delays, heartbreak or conflicts in your life—and you're getting discouraged. Friends, don't believe anything Satan shows or tells you; he is a liar. Remember that we live by faith, and not by sight. This is how the Holy Spirit guided me to defeat the spiritual attack in my life and taught me to take hold of the power and authority I have in Christ. When I fight spiritual battles with spiritual power, I always win.

When I experienced conflicts with people in high school, I never used to fight back. Instead I would go home and cry endlessly to my mother and persuade her to move me to another school. This continued year after year. During this time, I developed great hatred for myself and blamed myself for all my problems. This shaped me into a fearful, insecure, cowardly, people pleasing, prideful, perfectionistic, confused girl. You see, I was saved and baptized when I was thirteen years old and active in church, hungry for Jesus and trying to deepen my relationship with God. I was on the path of fulfilling my God given purpose. You can tell when great things are in you and ahead of you by how hard the enemy fights against you. Satan started attacking me as soon as I began my walk with Christ.

If we fast-forward a few years, as I got older and life got in the way, I drifted slightly away from the Lord, which was a big mistake. That's exactly what Satan wanted—to derail me from God's path for my life. That is exactly what he is trying to do in your life right now too, but he is about to lose because I am giving you the good news of God and will show you how to fight back through the help of the Holy Spirit.

Satan continued to attack me spiritually all the way into my adulthood. I experienced this problem at job after job—jealousy, envy, malice and pettiness always seemed to find me. As time passed, I hardened myself and decided to defend myself; I would try to take revenge and fight back, but even that was an epic fail. I was a wimp. My tears flowed often, and I just hated myself even more. I was allowing my human nature to lead me, and that never works.

Perhaps you are in a similar situation right now, experiencing a challenge but getting nowhere. If so, it's because you are approaching the problem using your own logic. So, instead of getting better, the situation gets even worse. I've been around that mountain a few times, and I can spare you the time and tell you that's not the way to go. I continued in my own strength for some time until I finally found my way back to God. He says He has given us the authority to trample on serpents and over all the power of the enemy through Christ Jesus, and I believe and live that out in my life even to this day.

I remember the season when the Holy Spirit dropped the revelation in my heart about how I should deal with the attacks I was experiencing. It was three years after I had recommitted my life to God and was building my relationship with Him. I was attending a Bible-based church that was teaching me the practicality of life in God, and I was having consistent fellowship with Him. I had just finished studying the first five books of the New Testament and was typing up my summarized notes on the chapters when the Holy Spirit dropped in my heart that I should emulate the behaviors of Jesus to deal with the situation with my co-workers. *"Follow His ways of dealing with conflicts and animosity,"* He told me, just as clear as day. I immediately looked up similar situations in the Bible. I felt like I had just solved world hunger—it was like a big light bulb went on. I remember saying to myself, "Ahhh, yes, that's right!"

You see, what was happening was that the Holy Spirit was influencing my mind and will, showing me how to die to my human nature and giving me direction to fight this attack spiritually. Before, I was fighting my own way—the way of the world—and I was having no success. The Holy Spirit opened up my spiritual eyes and made me understand what Satan had been doing to me for all those years, and He taught me how to win that battle once and for all. It wasn't my coworkers who were fighting against me; it was Satan and his demons influencing their behavior. *"For we are not fighting against human beings but against the wicked spiritual forces in the heavenly world, the rulers, authorities, and cosmic powers of this dark age."* (Ephesians 6:12, GNT). Friends, what you are experiencing right now is more than what your eyes can see. It's more than what they taught us in school. The answer to your problem can be found only in God. Don't bother wasting your time seeking a quick fix that will only bring on ten more attacks; go to the source, seek God and I guarantee you He will deliver you.

The Holy Spirit led me to every Scripture where Jesus had tension with the religious people so I could learn how Jesus handled it, but it was Romans 12:14-21 that put the icing on the cake for me. This Scripture details God's clear instructions for how to deal with opposition. The answer to every problem is in the Bible, whether you believe it or not. The Bible is called the wisdom book for a reason...the Bible is the oldest, most-used book in the world today for a reason. The Holy Spirit inspired me to read and study the passage in Romans day and night until it sank in. Those verses soon became my daily vitamins, and I put everything into practice that the Holy Spirit taught me.

Romans 12:14 says, *"Ask God to bless those who persecute you — yes, ask him to bless, not to curse."* While God was delivering me from this problem, He also helped me to die to myself and allow the Holy Spirit to lead me. I took this verse to heart and prayed every day for God to bless my co-workers and keep their families safe. I started practicing exactly what God instructed me to do. At first it was hard, but after a while I literally felt the transformation of humility within me.

Then I began living out Romans 12:17 and 18: *"If someone has done you wrong, do not repay him with a wrong. Try to do what everyone considers to be good. Do everything possible on your part to live in peace with everybody."* It's not easy to live in peace with someone who has made it their mission to fight you out of your bread and butter and make you uncomfortable. It's tough to love and respect them and treat them well. When I tried to do that in my own strength, I failed; so I made the decision to do things God's way instead of my own.

Friends, I can tell you that Satan did fight me over that— lies were told, and a number of people teamed up against me. I was definitely the odd man out, but I never paid that too much attention because I was fed up with doing things my way and allowing what I saw to lead me. I trusted God and let go of my own self; I humbled myself and continued to do good and forgive. I left everything to God, and I will tell you that God showed up for me big time. Every single person that was making my life miserable was removed from the company. I mean, one after the other, they were dismissed. I can testify that if you only trust God to take revenge for you, as He says in His Word He will do, and let Him deal with your situation, you will never be disappointed. And you can take that to the bank!

Soon after, I was promoted into a senior role in my company and had even more authority, leading and overseeing. God came through for me and rewarded me for obeying His laws and practicing righteousness; He taught me how to fight spiritually instead of how I had been going about it—which was like the world. And when I did, just like that, the power Satan used in spiritual attacks against me all those years backfired on him. It was shattered, destroyed, and can no longer hold me bondage. Right before my eyes, I saw myself beautifully transition from being led by my own carnal mind to being led by the spirit of God to victory.

Through this season, the Word of God was making progress in my life. I started to see myself in Christ; my dirt was being removed, and the born-again new person I am was coming through. The Holy Spirit showed me how to die daily to myself and allow the Holy Spirit to guide me. It was the most cleansing experience, though I must say it was hard at first. But that's normal because we are all born with a rebellious nature, but thanks be to God, the Holy Spirit did the work in me.

The Holy Spirit is your guide, and He can help you to spiritually fight those spiritual attacks the enemy is using against you. It doesn't matter what form the attack takes; God can do things that are impossible for man. He is beyond human wisdom and understanding. Get reconnected to God! Through obeying the leading of the Holy Spirit, I was able to defeat Satan over the spiritual attack he used on me for years—a problem I was trying to handle myself. But in one moment, the Holy Spirit shed light on it and set me free and this particular attack is no longer an issue for me. Obeying and surrendering to the Holy Spirit will mature you and bring you to new levels in your walk with God. I started trusting Him and very quickly learned to surrender to His leading. Nothing is so big or so small that the Holy Spirit will not help guide you through it; the Bible says He will lead you in all your ways.

For Your Quiet Time

1. Now that you understand what a spiritual attack is, what spiritual attacks have you been experiencing? List them.

   _____

   _____

   _____

   _____

   _____

2. Which Bible story or references in the Bible speak about what you are dealing with now?

   _____

   _____

   _____

   _____

   _____

   _____

3. Write out God's instructions about how you should deal with the problem. Pray about it and allow the Holy Spirit to direct you.

_____

_____

_____

_____

_____

_____

Guidance of the Holy Spirit

"I alone know the plans I have for you, plans to

bring you prosperity and not disaster, plans to

bring about the future you hope for."

(Jeremiah 29:11)

Life on my own was all about my own wisdom, my feelings and my five senses. I was involved in relationships that shouldn't have made it past hello, and experiences that should not have been part of my journey. Living life with God versus out of God is a night and day difference. Life without God is consciously choosing to hold yourself back from living your truest life and being the complete, whole person you were created to be. When doing life with God, you get complete access to the one who knows you best—God, your Creator, your Maker. He is your spiritual GPS; He'll tell you when to turn, where to turn, when to move and when not to move for your own safety.

He'll tell you who to marry, where to live, whether you should accept that business proposal, whether you should pursue that friendship. God will lead you in all your ways and give you insights to things you would never know with your own wisdom and five senses. God will amaze you. He will also share with you things that are about to take place in your life—whether blessings, favor or exposing the evil plans someone might have toward you and even your loved ones. God talks to us in various ways—through His words in the Bible, a vision, a sermon, a woman or man of God prophesying in your life or just a peace that God puts in your spirit.

As I grew in my relationship with God, He began to speak to me in different ways. Before, He would speak to me through the Bible or orchestrate relevant messages into my daily readings. For instance, I read the *Daily Bread* every day. God would often use those daily readings to communicate something to me or give me an answer concerning a situation or some question about which I was praying.

Several years ago, I was in the conversion stage and spending a lot of time with the Lord. At the same time, I was waiting for updates about my family's immigration status, which had been in process for the past twelve years. I doubted that I was going to be able to go with my family because of my age. When we first filed, I was a child; by the time the process was completed, I was an adult. At any rate, I was worrying a lot because I thought my name would be removed from the request and I wouldn't be able to join my family in moving to the US. I remember praying and giving it to God for His will to be done. I told God if it was His will for me to go, fine—but if not, then I trusted He had something better for me.

I had been praying this prayer for quite some time when I was reading my *Daily Bread* one day and the title of the message was "Your Flight Has Been Confirmed." On that very day, I received confirmation from the U.S. embassy that my family and I were confirmed for migration to the U.S. Needless to say, this strengthened my relationship with God even more, and I was amazed.

The Lord will speak to you in different ways. These days, He gives me visions. In the midst of passing through some testing, the Lord started to give me peeks behind the curtain regarding favors and blessings that were about to come in my life. Visions are similar to dreams; they come while you're sleeping or even while you're awake, and they portray events before they happen, just as they will happen. God has given me vision after vision about what is about to take place in my life.

Some years ago, the Lord favored me by giving me the chance to work on some great projects where I was employed; He provided opportunities I wasn't even looking for doing things I never knew I had a knack for. The Lord gave me a vision about the first project beforehand, and I thought, "Oh, okay, that would be nice." But I didn't give it much thought— assuming it was just a dream, until it actually happened. I continued to get visions about various events in my life and even about other people. I never experienced such things when I was living out of Christ; in fact, I was blind to most things. A few years ago, I emigrated from my home country of

Jamaica to America with my family. I settled in New York, while the rest of my family settled in Connecticut. I believe the Lord coordinated that because it was during this time by myself that I was tested about a number of different things that held me hostage, and the Lord taught me how to defeat those attacks.

My initial plan was to stay with relatives for three months at the most before branching out on my own. One evening as I was coming home from work, my head filled with plans and ideas about where I wanted to live, I was stopped in my tracks when I heard the Lord say to me, "You are going to be here for a little while." I was shocked. That instantly burst my independence bubble, but it turned out to be true; three months turned into almost four years. However, I was still a baby in my relationship with God at that point, so I didn't believe what I heard. In fact, I thought it was the enemy telling me foolishness because what God said was not in alignment with my plans.

Those four years were rough. During that time, I tried to branch out on my own and get my own place and establish my own roots, but it just never happened. On paper, I could have made it work, but I had no peace in my spirit about it. Every apartment I looked at just wasn't right; something was always wrong—whether the rent was too expensive, the place wasn't my style or it was too far from work. I also had a romantic interest in my life at the time, but God never allowed that relationship to move forward. I spent months trying to branch out on my own, and every time the Lord told me it wasn't yet time. A lot of animosity was going on in the home where I lived, and I was like meat in a lion's den. This was just one more reason why I wanted to be on my own.

I was sad, depressed, alone and disappointed—but God kept telling me that I must stay and go through it. I remember crying bitterly and begging God to change the circumstances, but nothing changed. The Lord just kept telling me to wait...to continue to go through the process. You see, I was a wimp; I was a coward and very fearful of people. I could hardly stand up for myself much less be bold and confident, so the Lord decided to use that time to eradicate those strongholds from my life. The Holy Spirit helped me to discern and understand God's plan during this season, and I became patient and was up for the ride even though it was difficult.

Friends, God came through for me, I obeyed Him every step of the way and saw Him take care of everyone that was fighting against me. It is the most amazing feeling and experience to see God defending you. It is so important to live by the leading of the Holy Spirit and allow Him to help you figure out your next move and what's best for you. Looking back, if I had never followed the leading of the Holy Spirit during that season in my life, I would never have dealt with an important inner issue, something that seriously needed to be addressed, residues of strongholds from my childhood.

Ultimately, I passed with flying colors all the tests that God sent my way, and my home situation became more peaceful. I had put getting my own place on a back burner because I was going through the tests, but eventually I realized that the test was over and the season had ended. The Lord started giving me discernment about making a faith move and getting my own place, ultimately stepping into a new season. But I was a bit confused about where I should live, so of course I sought directions from my Papa, God. I prayed and asked Him to show me what to do. I didn't get a complete answer immediately, but I discerned that He wanted me to step out in faith. Looking back, I see that God was fine-tuning the gift of discernment in me.

So, I started exploring my options. For a bit, I was thinking about moving to Atlanta, but that was an epic fail. I thought Atlanta would be a good place to lay roots because homes are affordable and I would have been able to get more for my money than where I was, so I visited. However, while the state is beautiful, it was not for me. The Lord made that very clear in the short time I was there, and I left feeling worse than when I arrived, because I really thought Atlanta was going to be it. I was confused and sad, continuing to cry to God bitterly, *Lord where do You want me to live? I know You want me to make a move; I can feel You impressing my spirit, but You haven't told me. I know it's not Atlanta or New York, so where?*

41

I questioned the Lord often, but still nothing. However, I just kept waiting for His instructions because He has always come through for me. Then one day I was having a conversation with my family in Connecticut—it was a conversation that we'd had often over the previous four years, but I never listened because it never made any sense. But on this occasion, God opened my eyes and ears to be ready to hear. You see, God had been doing some detail work on me over those four years and, even though the kitchen was very hot, I had to stay and allow Him to work on me. It hadn't been the right time to move...until now. Instantly my eyes opened, and I was able to see that moving to Connecticut was what God desired for me.

In July of 2017, I made the faith move to Connecticut. I left behind a growing career path with great opportunities to move into the unknown. But the beautiful thing about it is that I was so happy and expecting great things; fear was nowhere to be found in me, and I can tell you that God showed up for me. You see, all this time God had been planning and preparing the way

42

for me, and everything worked out beyond my expectations. Less than a month later, I had a job, a car and an apartment, and God gave me the best of everything. I now enjoy work and life balance, and everything else that I desired. God provided that and more; in fact, He wowed me to the max.

You see, God saved me from making what would have been a huge mistake, one I would have regretted if I had failed to trust His leading because I was so anxious and desperate. You may think, "Do I really need God to tell me where to live? I mean, if I make the wrong move, I will eventually recoup. This happens to people every day. What's the big deal?" Well, here is the deal: when you get out of line with God's plans for you, things will happen to you that shouldn't, sometimes even unfortunate things that can change your life or perhaps even cause your death. You can't go wrong following God's leading; you save time, energy, money and ultimately your life when you listen to His leading. He made you; He knows everything about you. Trust Him.

When you're spiritually connected to God, His will becomes your will; you know it, and you act accordingly — that is called discernment. Discerning God's will for you can save you from making bad decisions, like marrying the wrong person, making moves that you shouldn't, starting a business that won't succeed, and the list goes on and on. Discernment is knowing God's plan for you and doing it.

For Your Quiet Time

1. What is God inspiring in your life right now? (Career? Marriage?)

_____

_____

_____

_____

_____

_____

2. What are some of the ways that He spoke to you about this?

_____

_____

_____

_____

_____

_____

3. Do you have peace about it? Describe your peace.

_____

_____

_____

_____

_____

_____

Daddy!

"How great is the love the Father has lavished on us,

that we should be called children of God!"
(1 John 3:1)

No one can ever love you the way God loves you. He loves you with the agape kind of love. His love is unconditional; there is no "because of" to His love for you. You don't have to do anything to earn His love, and He still loves you even when you mess up. The very nature of Daddy is to love, and He wants to pour His love into your heart and into every area of your life. The moment you accept Jesus as your Lord and Savior, you are spiritually reconnected to Him.

God is our Father, and He must be viewed as our father figure. Just as an earthly father loves his child, teaches them right from wrong, comforts them, corrects and disciplines them, our Heavenly Father does the same. God is our Father, and we should not be afraid of Him, thinking that He is strict. I understand that many people misunderstand God because they don't take the time to know Him, but God is far from the aggressive persona you assume Him to be.

I remember in the early stages of my walk with the Lord, I desperately wanted to have my own perspective, my own experience of who God is. I felt that I needed to know Him myself and not simply see Him through the eyes of a pastor or Christian family member; I wanted my own encounter. I had already seen Him in so many different capacities in my life, and I guess I wanted to process all of it. One day while living in New York, riding the Number 2 train into Brooklyn for church, I remember praying and asking God to help me understand Him more. The Lord directed me to write down words that described who He was to me. I began writing: God is my teacher, God is my corrector, God is my friend, God is mysterious, God is my protector. As I wrote, tears began streaming down my face because every description had a story.

It was then I realized that God is my everything. That was a very powerful day—just God and me on the train—and the Holy Spirit spoke to me; all I could do was cry. God is your life partner, parent, friend, teacher—whoever you want Him to be, He is that and more. During my single season, I would go on vacation, go out to dinner and cook at home for God and me. I would check in to four-star hotels and enjoy myself just as I would have if I had company. Actually, I probably had more fun because having that alone time with God was very freeing. I stepped into candlelit restaurants and ordered some of the most luxurious dishes on the menu—for God and me. You see, God is my life partner first. Before my future husband, I need to have a relationship with God.

God can fill any need you have. Many times when I felt alone, I would just lift up my thoughts to who He is in my situations. He is my protector and guide; believing that truth and standing in it helped me through some rough times. And God will help you, too, if you believe.

As I mentioned, just a few years ago, I was living in a very uncomfortable environment. I was so fearful because I felt that I was at the mercy of the other people living in the house. I didn't understand at the time that God has authority over everything and can change any situation because he is God. I was so afraid of my housemates to the point that if I needed a drink and they were in the living room, I wouldn't go for a drink because I hated confrontations, animosity and problems; so I avoided them. I would often wait until everybody was asleep to leave my little space to get anything or do anything. During this season, the Lord was removing some weaknesses, fear and bondage that had held me hostage for years.

I remember one day when I was thirsty but refused to go get a drink because of my fear. I also remember the Lord dealing with me about how fearful I was. He said, "Do you trust Me? Don't you see that I am here with you? Nobody will ever touch you because I am with you. You are protected because I am here with you. Now get up and go get some water." The Lord instantly gave me confidence. I didn't even feel like myself. I literally felt the presence of God beside me, and it was so amazing. When I went into the kitchen to get the water, my housemates were all amazed because they knew I typically didn't dare come where they were.

I filled a glass, and the Lord told me to stand right there and drink it in front of them. Somewhat amazed, I obeyed. Then He told me to drink more—He knew I was ready to short myself just to get out of the room. I stood there drinking that second glass of water with the Lord by my side, and I started to feel a weight fall off of me; I was loosed from my fear, and the confidence of God filled me. I took my time, washed the glass, then walked calmly back to my room. I can tell you from that day forward, the bondage of fearing people was broken because of who God is to me. I chose to believe that He is my protector and guide. I held on to that promise, and He came through for me.

God is my teacher and mentor as well. He taught me how to believe in myself, and how to stop doubting myself and allowing other people to define me. He mentored me into becoming the bold, "God-fident" woman I am today. Those same people that were making my life miserable where I lived were eventually all removed from the house for one reason or another. Soon I had the entire place to myself and enjoyed peace and quiet. As that season of my life came to a close, the Lord blessed me bountifully to have my own place.

What in your life is trying to control you? Do you believe that God loves you and will be there for you? Walk and talk in that truth, and watch God work! God is our original parent. The parents you have by natural birth are the earthly parents that God, your original parent, gave the opportunity to bring you to the earth. So, it is God you should look to first to be a good parent to you. When our parents abandon us, pass away, hurt us or simply don't know how to be good parents, God—our first parent—will take care of us. He knows us more than we know ourselves because we are from Him. He knows secrets and desires that our earthly parents would have no idea about. Just as a good father knows his son, our heavenly Daddy knows us so well. God is patient with us and He is with us through all of life's hurdles. He uses our entire life to mature, mold, teach and correct us. He doesn't give us what we're not ready to handle. He prepares us for what we want before He gives it to us.

A hurt in your life could be that either your dad or mom is not in your life. No matter the case, I want to share a truth about you—God is your Father. I have my mother and father in my life, and I love them dearly; but God is my parent first before them. God is your Father, and He loves you more than your mind can comprehend. When your experiences in life have been rough and left scars you're trying to deal with even now, Satan continues to replay those experiences in your mind to discourage you. But God is seeing everything, and your pain hurts Him so much. He wants to help you, to free you from that pain, hurt, guilt and condemnation.

You see, pain, hurt, guilt and condemnation is all Satan has to offer; that's what he wants you to feel. But your heavenly Daddy can fix that. He can clean you up, wash you and make you whole, complete. Your past is your past, and that's all it is.

Everybody has one; stop beating yourself up. God's hands are wide open, waiting for you, but He cannot step in until you make the decision. God will never force anything on us, and that's why He made us with a will to choose. The moment you believe in Jesus Christ and what He did for you, I promise that you will never be the same again. God sent Jesus to pay for our sins through a substitutionary death. When Jesus died, the old you died with Him; and your new being rose with Him. You are forgiven of all your sins–past, present and future. You are justified, complete, free with God. God will break the generational curse off your life; He will fix you up and make you look like the person you should be in the first place. His arms are open wide, waiting for you to reconnect with Him by believing Jesus Christ.

Nothing on this earth can complete us except God. Our children, spouse, family and friends are only blessings from God to us. While our loved ones might turn their backs on us or pass away, God will never leave us; He is always present with us. He knows us more than we know ourselves. He can go into areas of our mind and heart that neither we nor anyone

else can access. God's love for us is out of this world!

For Your Quiet Time

1. How do you view God?

_____

_____

_____

_____

_____

_____

2. Describe a memorable encounter you had with God.

_____

_____

_____

_____

_____

_____

3. Make a list of words that describe God to you (based
   on your relationship with Him).

   _____

   _____

   _____

   _____

   _____

   _____

The Sanctification Process

"May the God who gives us peace make you holy in

every way and keep your whole being —spirit, soul

and body—free from every fault at the coming of

our Lord Jesus Christ."

(1 Thessalonians 5:23)

Once you understand the sanctification process, you'll dismiss
the myth that you're supposed to magically be a perfect
Christian overnight. You'll stop feeling discouraged when you
have occasional slipups, you'll stop feeling pressured to be
perfect instantly, you'll stop having feelings of failure and think
you have backslidden because of how many times you fail. The
very fact that you are aware of your sins means that you are
listening to the Holy Spirit.

Sanctification is the process of making holy, purifying from
defilement, abstaining from all sinful behavior (Matthew

5:1416). It is our way of showing love to God by yielding control of our lives to Him. It's an ongoing process that can be done only by the leading of the Spirit. It's learning to surrender and submit to Him, allowing God to increase in us while we decrease (John 3:30)

The truth is that we're all going through the sanctification process, not a condemnation process. It's okay to examine yourself and take inventory of your weaknesses and their root causes; but when you condemn yourself, God doesn't want that for you. Rather than staying in that place of error, ask for and receive forgiveness, then keep moving forward in God. Pray and ask the Lord to help you rebuke those unrighteous tendencies.

Two contending forces war within us as believers—the old nature and the new nature. The old nature we inherited from Adam, and that nature didn't disappear when we became Christians; it is still there. We have both the old nature we were born with that is fleshly and sinful (Romans 7:23-24) and the new nature, which is made in the image of God (Colossians 1:

27). The old nature is well formed, and the new nature is being formed.

Perhaps one of your biggest struggles is still being led by your old human nature instead of the new Spirit nature, still handling the situations of life the same way you did before the Spirit dwelled within you. Whatever you're going through, remember that the sanctification process is lifelong, not overnight. Stop pressuring yourself. Sanctification is honoring God, choosing daily to do things His way instead of yours. The more you let go and allow the Holy Spirit to work in you, the more you will see the almighty power, blessing and favor of God in your life. Sanctification is a beautiful process, depending on how you look at it. It's choosing to let go of yourself, releasing your earthly weapons and everything else in exchange for God.

What you need to understand is that you are always forgiven. When you made the decision to make Jesus your personal Savior, you were forgiven for all sins—past, present and future. You are justified because Christ paid all your debts so you don't need to stay in guilt and condemnation; all you need to do is confess. The Bible says he who the Son has set free is free indeed. That means every sin—yesterday, today and in the future.

The sanctification process is not always easy or pretty, but it's much-needed work—work that only the Holy Spirit can do in us. The process is like cleaning out an old house that has been abandoned for years. Over the years, the house has become dusty, overrun by rodents and infested with cobwebs. Have you ever watched those home makeover TV shows where the designer and the architect remodel a house—where they remove all the muck and replace it with new stuff? They always break down some of the walls to open up space and bring in natural light—the setup of the previous owner was often hiding the great potential of the home. Fresh paint works wonders, and the place looks totally different when the designers finish painting. Then the new furniture goes in, and the beauty of the home begins to shine even more. The house is transformed; you can barely see any remnant of the old house. The work that went in transformed it completely, making it brand new. This is what the Holy Spirit is doing in us right now!

Jesus Christ is the architect; He takes us up out of the dump and draws up the new plan. Then the Holy Spirit is like the builder who comes in and does the deep cleaning; He purifies us and makes us holy, removing our muck — selfishness, pride, anger, bitterness, rebellion, sexual immorality and insecurity — and replacing it with the fruit of the Spirit, aligning us with the will of God for our lives.

Our dysfunction comes in all different shapes and sizes, but is still similar. The common denominator is our sinful nature, the nature we inherited from Adam; but we must die to it every single day. The Holy Spirit is our helper, and He will help us in this transformation process; but we must choose to allow the Spirit to lead and not the body. Salvation is what we get from God when we repent, trust Christ and take Him as our personal Savior, while sanctification is what we give to God. It is when we choose to die to the sinful nature of our flesh and to receive correction and feed the spirit man daily.

Sanctification is a process of making holy, so I ask you, what is God working out in you now to make you more holy? He is always working on something. He might be speaking to you about a bad habit, places you're going, some toxic person you're hanging out with, television shows you watch or music you listen to that is planting seeds of lust, greed, fear, envy, materialism or other types of weeds in your heart. Yes, that is part of the sanctification process! Anything or anyone that is acting opposite to God's will is not helping your sanctification process. So watching a television show portraying a scantily clad woman committing adultery and cussing out her family is not a show a believer should be watching. You are planting bad seeds in your heart, then wondering why you're not growing.

You might say, "But, Shakira, I am not doing what they are doing in the shows. I know better." I know you do, but you are opening yourself up to demons associated with those activities; you're inviting those sins into your life. Did you ever watch a television show or listen to some music only to find that you feel like doing what you just watched or heard? If a food commercial can trigger hunger, why would you think television shows or music can't influence what you do? Choose to be led by the Spirit and not your body; decide to feed your spirit man with fellowship, the Word, the fruit of the Spirit and healthy, wholesome entertainment—not fleshly activities that will quench the Holy Spirit.

For me, one of the first things the Holy Spirit dealt with me about was letting go of my selfish way of standing up for myself. Having been bullied for some years, I grew up learning to fight back. The Holy Spirit checked me on that and made me realize that I needed to let go of the world's way and do things His way. I had to learn to bite my tongue, practice kindness, be patient and love those who were malicious toward me. God taught me to pray for those same people, asking Him to bless them. Letting go of the world's way was learning to forgive for real, admitting when I had lingering bitterness in my heart and allowing the Holy Spirit to help me forgive instead. I had to pray and ask Him to help me love my enemies, and through

Him I was surely able to do so (2 Corinthians 6:4-6). He will help you win your battles too.

When we become believers, we become new creatures through Christ Jesus; but that old nature we inherited from Adam is still with us. Every day, both natures are battling to lead us. We already know what the old nature is about and capable of, and that is the very reason why we let it go at Calvary—it is sinful and not of God. But it is our spirit that should lead us, our spirit that is being influenced by the Holy Spirit of God— and making the daily choice to be led of the Spirit comprises the lifelong sanctification process.

Sanctification doesn't happen magically. It requires rebuking our human ways daily and allowing the Spirit to lead us. We will fail, but we can't allow that to keep us down. Instead, we confess, receive forgiveness and move forward, allowing the Holy Spirit to work in us. The process must first take place on the inside before it shows on the outside, and we are all going through it. God loves us and knew we were going to have some falls, but He is right beside us, ready to pick us up and dust us off and set us on our way again. Daily fellowship and thanksgiving to the Lord will strengthen our spirit man and weaken our flesh. Stay in the fight, my friend.

For Your Quiet Time

1. In your own words, what is the sanctification process?

   _____

   _____

   _____

   _____

   _____

   _____

2. What is the Lord purifying in you right now? And how
   are you progressing?

   _____

   _____

   _____

   _____

   _____

   _____

3. What is the one thing you could be doing that is hindering your sanctification process? And what are you doing to rebuke it?

_____

_____

_____

_____

_____

_____

Quiet Time

"Instead, they find joy in obeying the law of the
Lord, and they study it day and night. They are like
trees that grow beside a stream."

(Psalms 1:2-3)

Quiet time is quality time you spend alone with God. It's an intimate time where you humbly go before God to open up your heart to Him and in return He opens up to you. Quiet time is a way of building your relationship with God. Here you find solutions to your problems and strength for your journey as you grow in love with God and develop the spirit of humility as you practice being still before Him. There is no set practice for what you should do in your quiet time; listen to the leading of the Holy Spirit, and He will guide you about what to do.

Quiet time for me varies. I always go by the leading of the

Holy Spirit, what is happening in my life or how I'm feeling on that day. I usually start off with just venting to God about my day—the good, bad and ugly. I am very transparent; I get everything off my heart and also get emotional and express my love to Him. It's very important that I am raw and honest; if I'm not, I won't get the help I need. So, I really "let go" to Him. Very often I will tell God about a problem I'm having (like He doesn't already know), and He will influence my mind and will regarding what to do. It's deep and different, I know, but this is what He does for me. After venting, I often find myself pausing as He gives me wisdom about the situation. Then I find myself speaking His instructions aloud. I love it when that happens. You see, God speaks to us in different ways; it's nice when He mixes it up. That keeps me on my toes; after all, we are in a relationship. On other occasions, the Holy Spirit will instruct me to read a particular chapter in the Bible, and it will turn out to be the words I need to hear to help me get out of my funk. During your intimate quiet time with God, you are free to be yourself—pour out your heart, be vulnerable, and just be transparent with Him.

On those days when I feel like negative situations aren't changing and I want to give up, I become a like little baby before Him, seeking comfort and assurance. Do you know what? I always get it, because I won't stop until I do. He will always lead me to Scriptures that give me comfort and top it off with peace and contentment in my spirit. In the next chapter, I share Scriptures He has given me that function like my own little comfy blanket.

You can even journal during your quiet time. Maybe sitting down and having a talk out loud with God is not your thing; in that case, you can journal. Write down what's on your heart. I approach this the same way as talking to Him. I pour out every single thing on my heart. God has a sense of humor. I remember one day I was writing about a situation that really annoyed me. I was distraught and definitely approaching the situation with my old nature; but the Holy Spirit called me out very quickly. After I finished venting about how I was feeling, I stopped writing to pause and listen. I had been journaling on my computer, and the Holy Spirit told me to change the color of the font to red and write out what He impressed on my heart. I thought that was hilarious and even got a good laugh from it, but I realized that God was dealing with me about the situation and I needed to listen and obey. He gave me the solution—though it wasn't what I wanted to hear—and He directed me in the right way to approach the situation that was affecting me.

You may be wondering how you can know it's God talking to you instead of just your own thoughts or Satan. You can discern this by checking whether what you are hearing aligns with the Word of God. For example, in this situation I mentioned, I was journaling in such a rebellious heat over the circumstances that I didn't realize I was approaching it with my selfish nature. But the Lord's wisdom instructed me to do good. Satan is not going to tell you to do good; he'll push you to do wrong and show you only how to make matters worse. God is love, peace and righteousness. Quiet time is powerful, a time when God can really speak to you and you will actually listen because it's just the two of you—no phones, no television and no friends.

Devotion is always a good element in your quiet time—it's a time to express your love and appreciation for God in the form of singing. You can go about this based on your own preferences. I've had a hymnbook for some years that contains songs that minister to my heart. Some of my favorites are "I Am Persuaded," "My Savior Lives," "Your Grace and Mercy," and "Spirit of the Living God." I enjoy singing to God. I also sing some of the modern praise and worship songs. Sometimes I play music on my smart TV or cell phone and sing along in worship to God. Music can bring me to a place where I am so captured in the worship that I don't even remember where I am; all I desire is Jesus. Allow music to minister to you in your quiet time with God.

One key to worshiping God is to give thanks for all He has done for you, think about what He has brought you through and delivered you from, and doors He has opened and still is opening. Think about how much He loves and cares for you.

Praise and worship are refreshing, but most important is showing honor to God. If necessary, search YouTube and Google to find music that ministers to you. Choose songs with lyrics that touch your heart.

Quiet time allows you to unwind with God; put aside your shyness and pride and share your heart with Him; He is waiting for you. Set a time and a place and make it habit to show up for that daily appointment. Did you know that God is eager for us to spend time with Him? It makes Him happy. He has things He wants to tell you and show you; He wants to give you glimpses of His plans for you. God loves you with an everlasting love; He craves your time and attention. Give it to Him.

For Your Quiet Time

1. What does quiet time with God mean to you?

_____

_____

_____

_____

_____

_____

2. How do you spend your quiet time?

_____

_____

_____

_____

_____

_____

3. What is one thing you would like to improve in your quiet time? And why do you think it needs improvement?

_____

_____

_____

_____

_____

Daily Vitamins

"You spoke to me, and I listened to every word. I

belong to you, Lord God Almighty, and so your

words filled my heart with joy and happiness."

(Jeremiah 15:16)

It all started a few years ago when the Holy Spirit led me to write down Scriptures to study to build up my spirit man. At the time the Holy Spirit was teaching me how to daily die to myself, so He led me to Scriptures that spoke to laying down the human nature and living by the Spirit. This was very effective for me, since it not only reminded me daily how to die to myself but also helped me study the Scriptures. Soon after, I started compiling Scriptures about everything; before long, whether it was a season I was in or a situation I was going through, I had Scriptures at my fingertips that spoke light to the situation. I would read them in the morning, afternoon and evening. Any time I found myself worrying or feeling less than a child of God, I would read them and remind myself of what God says about it. I always felt better; my spirit was lifted, my mind renewed as I took back the power and authority I have in Christ. I dubbed this activity my Daily Vitamins. Just like we take daily supplements to build, nourish and strengthen our bodies, similarly, I daily memorize Scriptures that I need to build my spirit man and help me power through each day. I want to share with you some of the Scriptures I use in various seasons to give me strength and remind me of the precepts of God; I pray you'll use these as building blocks to build your daily spiritual supplements.

Living like Jesus Christ

These verses helped me during the early stage when the Holy Spirit was teaching me how to die to my human nature self and allow the Spirit to lead me. These Scriptures felt like a deep wash; I was called out, dealt with and taught the righteous thing to do. Each time I read it, I felt fresh, clean, holy, brand new. Soon, dying to myself on a daily basis became easier.

1 Peter 2:1-2 – *Rid yourselves, then, of all evil; no more lying or hypocrisy or jealousy or insulting language. Be like newborn babies, always thirsty for the pure spiritual milk, so that by drinking it you may grow up and be saved.*

James 4:11 – *Do not criticize one another, my brothers and sisters. If you criticize fellow-Christians or judge them, you criticize the Law and judge it. If you judge the Law, then you are no longer one who obeys the Law, but one who judges it.*

Colossians 3:8 – *But now you must get rid of all these things: anger, passion, and hateful feelings. No insults or obscene talk must ever come from your lips.*

Ephesians 4:29 – *Do not use harmful words, but only helpful words, the kind that build up and provide what is needed, so that what you say will do good to those who hear you.*

Ephesians 4:2 – *Be always humble, gentle, and patient. Show your love by being tolerant with one another.*

Philippians 2:3 – *Don't do anything from selfish ambition or from a cheap desire to boast, but be humble towards one another, always considering others better than yourselves.*

Romans 12:1 – *So then, my brothers and sisters, because of God's great mercy to us I appeal to you: offer yourselves as a living sacrifice to God, dedicated to his service and pleasing to him. This is the true worship that you should offer. Do not conform yourselves to the standards of this world but let God transform you inwardly by a complete change of your mind. Then you will be able to know the will of God, what is good and is pleasing to him and is perfect.*

Proverbs 16:24 – *Pleasant words are as a honeycomb, sweet to the soul, and health to the bones.*

Philippians 4:8 – *Fill your minds with those things that are good and deserve praise: things that are true, noble, right, pure, lovely and honorable.*

Ephesians 4:22 – *So get rid of your old self, which made you live as you used to – the old self that was being destroyed by its deceitful desires. Your hearts and minds must be made completely new.*

Practicing and nourishing our spirit man with the fruits of the spirit

We daily feed our body food for energy and nutrients; it is even more important that we daily feed our spirit man. We feed our spirit man not by eating natural foods like oranges, broccoli, and potatoes, but by practicing the acts of love, joy, peace, long suffering, goodness, kindness, humility, patience and self-control. Feeding your spirit man requires choosing to not retaliate to someone who is unkind to you or loving someone who hates you. Every time you choose to do what the Spirit influences you to do, you're nourishing your spirit man. These Scriptures daily reminded me how to nourish my spirit man.

Galatians 5: 22-23 – *But the spirit produces love, joy, peace, kindness, goodness, faithfulness, patience, humility and self control.*

Romans 12:12 – *Let your hope keep you joyful, be patient in your troubles and pray at all times.*

Romans 12:13 – *Share your belongings with your needy fellow Christians and open your homes to strangers.*

Romans 12:14 – *Ask God to bless those who persecute you. Yes, ask him to bless, not to curse.*

Romans 12:16 – *Have the same concern for everyone. Do not be proud, but accept humble duties. Do not think of yourselves as wise.*

Romans 12:17 – *If someone has done you wrong, do not repay him with a wrong. Try to do what everyone considers to be good. Do everything possible on your part to live in peace with everybody.*

Romans 12:21 – *Do not let evil defeat you, instead conquer evil with good.*

1 John 4:7 – *Let us love one another, because love comes from God. Whoever loves is a child of God and knows God.*

Colossians 3:14 – *And to all these qualities add love, which binds all things together in perfect unity.*

Hebrews 12:14 – *Make every effort to live in peace with everyone and to be holy; without holiness no one will see the Lord.*

Strength and encouragement

These Scriptures are my soft, comfy blanket on those dreary days when I feel blah or sad for whatever reasons. I usually turn to these verses to lift up my spirit, to revitalize, refresh and reset my mind. We all need that every now and then. This is your pick-me-up!

Isaiah 43:18-19 – *But the Lord says, do not cling to the things of the past or dwell on what happened long ago. Watch out for the new thing I am going to do. It is happening already; you can see it now! I will make a road through the wilderness and give your streams of water there.*

Isaiah 41:13 – *For I the Lord your God, hold your right hand; it is I who say to you, Fear not, I am the one who helps you.*

Philippians 4:19 – *For my God shall supply all my needs according to his riches in glory through Christ Jesus.*

Philippians 1:28 – *Don't be afraid of your enemies; always be courageous and this will prove to them that they will lose and that you will win, because it is God who gives you the victory.*

Isaiah 40:31 – *But those who trust in the LORD for help will find their strength renewed. They will rise on wings like eagles; they will run and not get weary; they will walk and not grow weak.*

Proverbs 18:10 – *The Lord is a strong tower, where the righteous can go and be safe.*

Psalms 1:3 – *I am like trees that grow beside a stream, that bear fruit at the right time and whose leaves do not dry up. I succeed in everything I do.*

Matthew 11:28 – *Come to me, all of you who are tired from caring heavy loads and I will give you rest.*

Psalms 115:105 – *Your word is a lamp under my feet and a light for my path.*

1 Peter 5:6-7 – *Humble yourselves, then under God's mighty hand, so that he will lift you up in his own good time. Leave all your worries with Him, because he cares for you.*

Singleness

The single season is an exciting time, but it can also be challenging, especially if you're in the season for a while. Watching your friends getting married and having children while you're not even dating can be rough. These Scriptures reminded me of God's precepts on how I should handle myself as a Christian single woman and assured me that He sees my heart and is orchestrating things. They encouraged me to focus on my purpose and trust Him to bring my future husband and me together.

2 Corinthians 6:14 – *Do not try to work together as equals with unbelievers, for it cannot be done. How can right and wrong be partners? How can light and darkness live together?*

Isaiah 54:5 – *God is my husband—the LORD Almighty is his name. The holy God of Israel will save me—he is the ruler of all the world.*

Colossians 3:3 – *For I am dead to lust and alive and well in Christ Jesus.*

1 Corinthians 6:18 – *Flee from sexual immorality. Every other sin a person commits is outside the body, but the sexually immoral person sins against his own body.*

Hebrews 13:4 – *Let marriage be held in honor among all, and let the marriage bed be undefiled, for God will judge the sexually immoral and adulterous.*

1 Thessalonians 4:3-5 – *For this is the will of God, your sanctification: that you abstain from sexual immorality; that each one of you know how to control his own body in holiness and honor, not in the passion of lust like the Gentiles who do not know God.*

Matthew 6:32-33 – *Your father in heaven knows that you need all these things. Instead, be concerned above everything else with the Kingdom of God and with what he requires of you, and he will provide you with all these other things.*

Genesis 2:18 – *Then the Lord God said, "It is not good that the man should be alone; I will make him a helper fit for him.*

1 Corinthians 7:21 – *I would like you to be free from worry. An unmarried man concerns himself with the Lord's work, because he is trying to please the Lord.*

Songs of Solomon 3:5 – *Promise me, women of Jerusalem; swear by the swift deer and the gazelles that you will not interrupt our love.*

Spiritual warfare

From time to time Satan and his little demons will try to oppress us. I usually pray these Scriptures and rebuke them with the authority I have in Christ.

Isaiah 59:18 – *According to their deeds, accordingly he will repay, fury to his adversaries, recompense to his enemies; to the islands he will repay recompense.*

Deuteronomy 28:13 – *And the Lord shall make thee the head, and not the tail; and thou shalt be above only, and thou shalt not be beneath.*

Luke 10:19 – *Behold, I have the authority to trample on serpents and scorpions and over all the power of the enemy and nothing shall by any means hurt me.*

Isaiah 54:17 – *No weapon formed against me shall prosper and every tongue which raises against me in judgment shall be condemned. This is the heritage of the servants of the Lord and their righteousness is from Me, says the Lord.*

Psalms 144:1 – *Blessed be the Lord my strength, which teaches my hands to war and my fingers to fight.*

1 John 4:4 – *But you belong to God, my children; and have defeated the false prophets; because the spirit who is in you is more powerful than the spirit in those who belong to the world.*

Deuteronomy 31:6 – *Be determined and confident. Do not be afraid of them. Your God, the LORD himself, will be with you. He will not fail you or abandon you.*

Galatians 5:1 – *Freedom is what we have—Christ has set us free! Stand then; as free people, and do not allow yourselves to become slaves again.*

Isaiah 41:10 – *Fear not, for I am with you; be not dismayed, for I am your God; I will strengthen you, I will help you, I will uphold you with my righteous right hand.*

Hebrew 4:12 – *The word of God is alive and active, sharper than any double-edged sword. It cuts all the way through to where the soul and spirit meet, to where joints and marrow come together.*

My identity in Christ

These Scriptures will remind you of who you are in Christ on those days when the enemy tries to tell you otherwise. You are a new creature; the old you is gone. You are a child of God.

1 John 4:16 – *And we ourselves know and believe the love which God has for us.*

Colossians 2:10 – *You have been given full life in union with him. He is supreme over every spiritual ruler and authority.*

Ephesians 2:5 – *That while we were spiritually dead in disobedience he brought us to life with Christ. It is by God's grace that you have been saved.*

Romans 8:2 – *For law of the spirit, which brings us life in union with Christ Jesus, has set me free from the law of sin and death.*

Ephesians 1:4 – *Even before the world was made, God had already chosen us to be his through our union with Christ, so that we would be holy and without fault before him.*

Colossians 3:9-10 – *I have put off the old man and have put on the new man, which is renewed in the knowledge after the image of Him Who created me.*

Luke 6:38 – *I have given, and it is given to me; good measure, pressed down, shaken together, and running over, men give into my bosom.*

John 15:5 – *I am the vine and you are the branches. Those who remain in me and I in them will bear much fruit, for you can do nothing without me.*

John 15:7 – *If you remain in me and my words remain in you then you will ask for anything you wish and you shall have it.*

1 Peter 2:9 – *But you are the chosen race, the King's priests; the holy nation, God's own people, chosen to proclaim the wonderful acts of God, who called you of darkness into his own marvelous light.*

Obligation to each other

The Lord made me understand the importance of serving, inspiring and honoring others. We should never allow someone's behavior to dictate how we treat that person. We must be patient and tolerant of our brothers and sisters, and even unbelievers. These Scriptures helped to humble me in this area.

Romans 15:1-3 – *We who are strong ought to bear with the failings of the weak and not please ourselves. Each of us should please our neighbors for their good, to build them up. For even Christ did not please himself but, as it is written, "The insults of those who insult you have fallen on me."*

Romans 13:8 – *Be under obligation to no one – the only obligation you have is to love one another. (Forgive, be patient, grace, mercy, kind, compassionate, be fair)*

91

Matthew 22:9 – *The second most important commandment is like it: 'Love your neighbor as you love yourself.'*

Colossians 3:13 – *Be tolerant with one another and forgive one another whenever any one of you has a complaint against someone else.*

Acts 20:28 – *So keep watch over yourselves and over all the flock which the Holy spirit has placed in your care. Be shepherd of the church of God, which he made his own through the blood of his Son.*

Hebrews 13:16 – *Do not forget to do good and to help one another, because these are the sacrifices that pleases God.*

John 15:12 -*My commandment is this: love one another, just as I love you.*

Luke 6:38 – *Give to others, and God will give to you. Indeed, you will receive a full measure a generous helping, poured into your hands – all that you can hold. The measure you use for others is the one that God will use for you*

Galatians 5 :14 – *For the whole Law is summed up in one commandment: "Love your neighbor as you love yourself."*

1 Peter 3:8 - *to conclude: you must all have the same attitude and the same feelings; love one another, and be kind and humble with one another.*

God loves me

These Scriptures are so precious to me. Every time I read them, I feel the love of God hugging me—it's powerful!

Zephaniah 3:17 – *The Lord your God is with you; his power gives you victory. The Lord will take delight in you and in his love, he will give you new life. He will sing and be joyful over you.*

Jeremiah 29:11 – *I alone know the plans I have for you, plans to bring you prosperity and not disaster, plans to bring about the future you hope for.*

Romans 5:8 – *But God has shown us how much he loves us – it was while we were still sinners that Christ dies for us!*

John 15:9- *I love you just as the Father loves me; remain in my love.'*

Psalms 17:7 – *Reveal your wonderful love and save me, at your side I am safe from my enemies.*

1 John 3:1 – *See how much the Father has loved us! His is so great that we are called God's children – and so, in fact, we are. This is why the world does not know is: it has not known God.*

Psalms 86:15 – *But you, O Lord, are a merciful and loving God, always patient, always kind and faithful.*

Romans 8:37-39 – *No one in all these things we have complete victory through him who loved us! For I am certain that nothing can separate us from his love: neither death, nor life, neither angels no other heavenly rulers or powers, neither the present nor the future, neither the word above nor the world below there is nothing in all creation that will ever be able to separate us from the love of God which is ours through Christ Jesus our Lord.*

Psalms 136:26 – *Give thanks to the God of heaven is love is eternal.*

Isaiah 43:2 – *When you pass through deep waters, I will be with you; your troubles will not overwhelm you. When you pass through the fire, you will not be burned, the hard trials that comes will not hurt you.*

For Your Quiet Time

1. What are your top five Scriptures?

   _____

   _____

   _____

   _____

   _____

   _____

2. In what areas in your life could you practice using more

   Scriptures?

   _____

   _____

   _____

   _____

   _____

   _____

3. What is the one Scripture that gives you the most comfort?

_____

_____

_____

_____

_____

_____

I want to hear from you

I know you have been blessed by this message. I'd like to continue to help you! Send your emails to,

shakira@life-withgod.com

Made in the USA
Las Vegas, NV
04 June 2021